A DOG'S LIFE

A journal for you and your pet
By Henry Horenstein
Illustrated by Pierre Le-Tan

A POND PRESS BOOK

MACMILLAN PUBLISHING COMPANY
New York
COLLIER MACMILLAN PUBLISHERS
London

Macmillan Publishing Company
866 Third Avenue, New York, N.Y. 10022
Collier Macmillan Canada, Inc.

ISBN 0-02-063240-1

Macmillan books are available at special discounts for bulk purchases
for sales promotions, premiums, fund-raising, or educational use.
For details, contact:

Special Sales Director
Macmillan Publishing Company
866 Third Avenue
New York, N.Y. 10022

10 9 8 7 6 5 4 3 2 1

Printed in Italy

This book is dedicated to
Jenny — and, of course, to
Dolly, Chammie I,
Chammie II, Chammie III,
Chammie IV, Snuffy,
Dobie, Pete, Emma,
Chamois, Sadie, and Jake

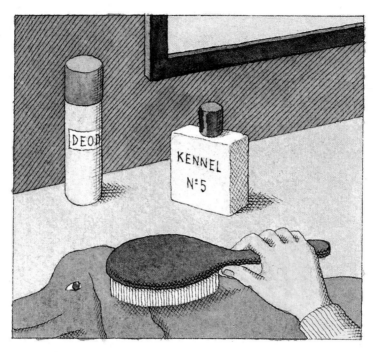

At the groomer's

Veterinarians

_____

Psychiatrist

Dogcatcher

Groomer

Sitters/walkers

_____

Feed store

Kennel

_____

Other

THE NEW ARRIVAL
Basic facts and first impressions
of your new pet

Name   Sex

Nickname

Date and time of arrival

Birthday

Source — where the dog came from

Color and markings

Weight

Size (shoulder to ground)

General health

Litter size (if known)

First impressions — your dog's and yours

Date   _Location_

Family tree

Breed — pedigree

Breed — cross between

Registered name

Registration number

Registered litter number

Breeder and breeder's address

Sire

Grand sire (sire)

Grand dam (sire)

Dam

Grand sire (dam)

Grand dam (dam)

Awards/ribbons

PAPERS

Your dog's pedigree or adoption papers —
and any awards or ribbons

Paper training

RITES OF PASSAGE
*Important events in a young dog's life —
where, when, and how they happened*

Remained quiet all night

Was neutered

Was house trained

First lifted leg

Went into heat

Lost virginity

Fought first fight

Chased cat or squirrel

Caught skunk

Attacked by porcupine

Stayed away from home all night

Other

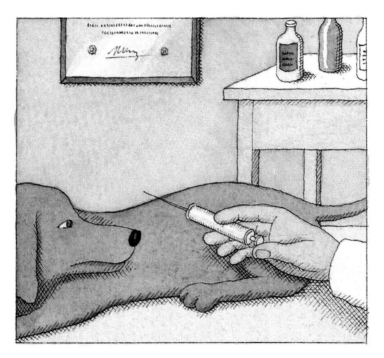

Visiting the vet

Date

Doctor/clinic

Ailment

Diagnosis

Treatment

Date

Doctor/clinic

Ailment

Diagnosis

Treatment

MEDICAL JOURNAL

Date

Doctor/clinic

Ailment

Diagnosis

Treatment

Date

Doctor/clinic

Ailment

Diagnosis

Treatment

Date

Doctor/clinic

Ailment

Diagnosis

Treatment

Date

Doctor/clinic

Ailment

Diagnosis

Treatment

Date   Location

Date

Doctor/clinic

Ailment

Diagnosis

Treatment

Date

Doctor/clinic

Ailment

Diagnosis

Treatment

MEDICAL JOURNAL

Date

Doctor/clinic

Ailment

Diagnosis

Treatment

Date

Doctor/clinic

Ailment

Diagnosis

Treatment

Date

Doctor/clinic

Ailment

Diagnosis

Treatment

Date

Doctor/clinic

Ailment

Diagnosis

Treatment

Taking medications

	Date	Date	Date	Date	Date	Date
Booster						
Distemper						
Heartworm						
Infectious hepatitis						
Leptospirosis						
Parainfluenza						
Parvovirus						
Rabies						

young dog

THE EARLY YEARS

Remembrances of your dog as a puppy

Date   _Location_

Dog in love

FIRST LOVE
The first object of your dog's affection

Name   *Species*

Owner (if applicable)

Your dog's behavior

the well-mannered dog

☐ *Obedient*   ☐ *Amusing*   ☐ *Uncomplaining*   ☐ *Comforting*
☐ *Intelligent*   ☐ *Sympathetic*   ☐ *Forgiving*   ☐ *Other*

Date   Location

Destructive dog

☐ *Won't come when called*
☐ *Chews furniture*
☐ *Starts fights*
☐ *Begs for food*
☐ *Runs away*
☐ *Attracts fleas and ticks*
☐ *Is always in the way*
☐ *Acts territorially*

☐ *Drinks toilet water*
☐ *Barks incessantly*
☐ *Chases cats*
☐ *Sheds excessively*
☐ *Jumps up on people*
☐ *Eats garbage*
☐ *Digs holes*
☐ *Throws up in car*

☐ *Sniffs crotches*
☐ *Sleeps on furniture*
☐ *Bites strangers*
☐ *Has bad breath*
☐ *Chases cars or bicycles*
☐ *Passes gas*
☐ *Shows relentless affection*
☐ *Licks faces*

the attentive dog

- ☐ *No*
- ☐ *Bark*
- ☐ *Stay*
- ☐ *Heel*
- ☐ *Come*

- ☐ *Down*
- ☐ *Speak*
- ☐ *Fetch*
- ☐ *Beg*
- ☐ *Out*

- ☐ *Play dead*
- ☐ *Roll over*
- ☐ *Shake*
- ☐ *Sit*
- ☐ *Walk*

- ☐ *Ball*
- ☐ *Stick*
- ☐ *None of the above*

Searching for the way home

LOST DOG
*Your dog's adventures while lost or
running away from home*

Dates of journey

Where found

How found

Condition when recovered

Dates of journey

Where found

How found

Condition when recovered

Date   Location

Dates of journey

Where found

How found

Condition when recovered

Dates of journey

Where found

How found

Condition when recovered

chasing a stick

☐ *Shake hands*   ☐ *Beg*   ☐ *Play tug of war*   ☐ *Other*

☐ *Catch the frisbee*   ☐ *Bark on cue*   ☐ *Sing*

☐ *Roll over*   ☐ *Heel*   ☐ *Play dead*

☐ *Chase the stick*   ☐ *Fetch the ball*   ☐ *Walk with leash in mouth*

the socially graceful dog

- ☐ Affectionate
- ☐ Clever
- ☐ Smart
- ☐ Frantic
- ☐ Calm
- ☐ Aggressive
- ☐ Devoted
- ☐ Stubborn
- ☐ Gentle

- ☐ Relentless
- ☐ Spoiled
- ☐ Deferential
- ☐ Ingratiating
- ☐ Lazy
- ☐ Bored
- ☐ Dignified
- ☐ Good-natured
- ☐ Attentive

- ☐ Frisky
- ☐ Loud
- ☐ Shy
- ☐ Fawning
- ☐ Neurotic
- ☐ Obnoxious
- ☐ Pushy
- ☐ Manic
- ☐ Reserved

- ☐ Wimpy
- ☐ Quiet
- ☐ Sensitive
- ☐ Inquisitive
- ☐ Silly
- ☐ Other

Date _____ _Location_ _____

Middle-aged dog

THE PRIME OF LIFE
*Remembrances of your
dog's middle years*

Dog delivery

☐ Guards property   ☐ Rescues strangers   ☐ Points out birds   ☐ Provides emotional support
☐ Protects children   ☐ Tracks down criminals   ☐ Delivers newspaper   ☐ Other
☐ Entertains guests   ☐ Herds sheep   ☐ Fetches slippers
☐ Races at the track   ☐ Hunts animals   ☐ Acts as a guide dog

_____   _____
Date   *Location*
_____

Tucking in the pups

Mate's name

Delivery date

Number in litter

Favorites

Homes for the puppies

Mate's name

Delivery date

Number in litter

Favorites

Homes for the puppies

Date   Location

Mate's name

Delivery date

Number in litter

Favorites

Homes for the puppies

Mate's name

Delivery date

Number in litter

Favorites

Homes for the puppies

THE PARENTAL DOG

Mate's name

Delivery date

Number in litter

Favorites

Homes for the puppies

Mate's name

Delivery date

Number in litter

Favorites

Homes for the puppies

Date   Location

Living the good life

- [ ] Eat
- [ ] Sleep
- [ ] Be scratched

- [ ] Play
- [ ] Go for a car ride
- [ ] Bark

- [ ] Lie on furniture
- [ ] Chew
- [ ] Be groomed

- [ ] Swim
- [ ] Go for a walk

☐ *Licks faces*
☐ *Wags tail*

☐ *Barks*
☐ *Snores soundly*

☐ *Rolls over*
☐ *Jumps up*

_____

_____

_____

_____

_____

_____

_____

_____

_____

_____

_____

_____

Strutting his stuff

Color and Markings

Build

Coat

Eyes

Ears

Tail

Muzzle

Legs

Eyebrows

Other

Date   _Location_

THE GOOD-LOOKING DOG

Date   _Location_

A dog retires

THE GOLDEN YEARS
Remembrances of your elderly dog

Date   _Location_

Scratching the dog

☐ *Unlimited biscuits*
☐ *Room in the middle of the bed*
☐ *Regular massage*
☐ *Table scraps*

☐ *Exercise and games*
☐ *Pep talks*
☐ *Hands and face for licking*
☐ *Visits to friends and family*

☐ *Rides in the car*
☐ *Other*

_____

_____

_____

_____

_____

_____

_____

_____

_____

_____

_____

Date   Location

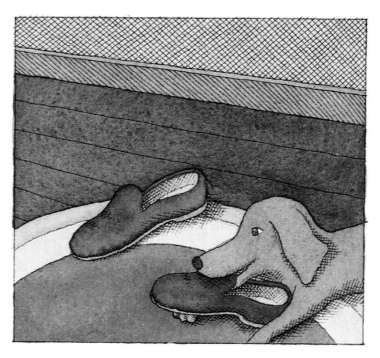

Chewing slippers

FAVORITE THINGS

Places or objects your dog especially likes
— where they are located and why they
are particularly favored

Armchair

Fireplace

Slippers or shoes

Neighbor's lawn

Laps

Rug

Garbage cans

Pond

Walking path

Shade tree

Other

Date　　　　　　　_Location_

A dog's best friend

BEST FRIEND
*People or animals, other than you,
that your pet likes most*

Name

Address

Sex   Species

Favorite games/activities

Date _____ _Location_ _____

Cowering as the lightning strikes

- ☐ Car backfire
- ☐ Firecrackers
- ☐ Street grates
- ☐ Thunder
- ☐ Lightning

- ☐ Flash from a camera
- ☐ Disapproval
- ☐ Punishment
- ☐ Loneliness
- ☐ Other animals

- ☐ Groomer
- ☐ Veterinarian
- ☐ Other

LOCK OF HAIR/MEMORABILIA

A lock of your dog's hair and any other memorabilia, such as old licenses, certificates, and name tags

LOCK OF HAIR/MEMORABILIA

Date   _Location_

Henry Horenstein is a writer and photographer. He is the author of several books, including Black and White Photography, *and is on the faculty of the Rhode Island School of Design.*

Pierre Le-Tan is a humorist and illustrator whose work appears in The New Yorker *and other periodicals, and in books, including John Train's* Remarkable Names of Real People. *Mr. Le-Tan lives with his numerous family in Paris and London.*

Art Direction: Lisa DeFrancis/Boston Designers: Lisa DeFrancis, Melissa Cohen Printed in Italy by Arnoldo Mondadori Editore